BALI

MORNING OF THE WORLD

Photography by Luca Invernizzi Tettoni

Text by Nigel Simmonds

PERIPLUS EDITIONS

Published by Periplus Editions (HK) Ltd

Copyright © 1999 Periplus Editions (HK) Ltd

Second printing, 1999

Publisher: Eric Oey
Editor: Kim Inglis
Production: Mary Chia, Violet Wong

Distributors:

Asia Pacific:
Berkeley Books Pte. Ltd.
5 Little Road, #08-01, Singapore 536983

Indonesia:
Pt. Wira Mandala Pustaka (Java Books–Indonesia)
Jl. Kelapa Gading Kirana, Block A14, No 17, Jakarta 14240

Japan:
Tuttle Publishing.
RK Bldg. 2nd Floor, 2-13-10 Shimo-Meguro, Meguro-Ku,
Tokyo 153 0064

USA:
Charles E. Tuttle Co., Inc.
RRI Box 231-5, North Clarendon, VT 05759-9700

Right: *Wayang kulit*, the shadow puppet play. To pass beyond this simple cloth screen is to enter Bali's enchanting world of spirits and demons.
Opposite: Sunrise at Sanur, with the sacred Mount Agung in the background. It was Pandit Nehru, India's first prime minister, who first called Bali the "Morning of the World".

CONTENTS

"The road ran on and on, a wide avenue between stone walls. Everywhere temples lifted their stone gates, carved as feathery as the banyan trees above them. The villages were miles of walls, thatched against the rain, with hundreds of prim pillared porticos, and groups of damsels sitting by them. Beyond those parapets were homes. What sort of people lived there? What manner of life did they lead behind their sheltering barriers?"

Hickman Powell,
The Last Paradise, 1930

INTRODUCTION

For four years I have lived in Bali. I arrived on holiday with very little knowledge of the "Island of the Gods"—when I stepped off the Garuda jumbo jet in October 1992 I knew next to nothing of its religion, had only a vague conception of its immense beauty and no real understanding of the extraordinary manner in which its people organize their lives. Today I feel lucky to have experienced an island which remains remarkable in a thousand different ways.

I knew this much at that time: many before me had been charmed by Bali's powerful magic. Hickman Powell, a 1930s visitor, called it "a vast spreading wonderland" and "the embodied dreams of pastoral poets". To the writer and musicologist Colin McPhee, another early fan, it exhibited a "golden freshness",

where everyone was either a dancer or an artist. Pandit Nehru—India's first prime minister—immortalized the island in the 1950s when he called it the "Morning of the World", a kind of tropical Garden of Eden where, according to another early description, "care-free islanders" lived as "happy as mortals can be". Could Bali really be this good, I wondered?

I began to find out on my first visit. Setting off from the artists' town of Ubud in the grassy central lowlands, a companion and I drove through the glaucous pre-dawn twilight to watch the sun rise over Mount Batur. As we emerged onto the lip of a long-defunct crater, within which stretched a vast volcanic valley, a single purple cloud hovered over a glassy lake like a fanciful addition to an already celestial scene. And then the sun exploded above us in a blush of soft carmine hues, and I was torn between a feeling of magical wonder, of being present on the day the world was born, and an idea of what it must be like to spend a lifetime blind, and then see colour and shape for the first time. "What is this place?", I remember thinking.

As if we needed more, the island handed us an even greater spectacle. Driving back to a recently rented thatched house in the rice fields, we were greeted by a pageant of colourfully costumed worshippers tripping their way through the dazzling green landscape to a twirly-edged temple in the distance. Dressed in white and yellow, hot orange and bright blue, a magnificent parade of Balinese women walked in front of an ornately carved golden sedan chair, its occupant a boy of no more than 10 years.

Behind this little king, with his adult gaze and regal persona, trouped brown-skinned and black-haired men, their features smooth and manner proud. And then more—a line of teenage girls, a vision of collective beauty descending in size right down to a last little toddler, a perfect copy in miniature of the first skinny, bejewelled girl. We sat entranced in our jeep on the side of the road and were captivated by the beat of Bali's hypnotic drum.

As life progressed I learned more about the culture of Bali. I learned that children were carried everywhere, held in the protective arms of a family member until three months old. I listened as a priest, dressed in white, chanted a mantra in an ancient language, and watched while an entire village clasped its palms together in prayer. I marvelled at the vibrant offerings prepared for the temple, and the simple gesture of a welcome smile. I saw dance and dramas to evoke the spirits, and shadows that fired the imagination. I learned to love the island.

Previous page: The lotus, the frangipani and an ornately carved temple gate in Ubud... a heady trinity which many believe still puts Bali above other Asian destinations.
Opposite: Pura Ulun Danu Bratan, the temple of the Lake goddess near Bedugul in north Bali.
Below: Festival offerings for the gods.

Above: Bali's rugged eastern mountains viewed from Kintamani.
Opposite: *Jukung* – traditional Balinese fishing boats.

These days, I understand Bali a little better than I did on that first early morning in Batur—like a wised-up city boy initially enamoured with the country farm, I now recognize an earthly pragmatism which goes beyond the geographic splendour of rural living. Life is not easy for everybody on Bali. Their deep and sensual religion offsets the daily hardship of a lifestyle that in many quarters remains largely unchanged since the 17th cen-

tury. Yet I continue to recognize within the culture an extra-ordinary sense of community, one which transcends our Western ideals of liberty and individualism and puts coopera-tion above competition. This, perhaps more than anything else, is the real substance of Bali's beauty. It is an island populated by a people who know how to live together. Few cultures can say the same, even though many may try.

Left and right: "No feast is complete in Bali," wrote the Mexican expatriate Miguel Covarrubias in 1937, "without music and elaborate dramatic and dance performances; no one would dream of getting married, or holding a cremation, or even of celebrating a child's birthday, without engaging troupes of dancers and actors to entertain the guests and neighbours." Dance and drama remain central to the Balinese way, colourful spectacles in the life of the culture. In fact Covarrubias and his wife became such enthusiastic theatre-goers during their time on the island they "sometimes had to make a point of staying home to catch up with lost sleep". The Mexican chronicler wrote in his still definitive book, *Island of Bali*: "Even the tired peasant who works all day in the fields does not mind staying up at night to watch a show, and the little children who invariably make up the front rows of the audience remain there until dawn for the end, occasionally huddled together taking naps, but wide awake for the exciting episodes of the play." Next to having good orchestras, a fine group of dancers is an imperative need for the spiritual and physical well-being of the community. When a society has enough money for the elaborate costumes needed for public appearance, the village *banjar* or community association gives an inauguration festival to bless the clothes. All actors, dancers or story-tellers undergo the same ceremony—in the case of a dancer, a priest uses the stem of a flower to inscribe magic syllables on the face, head, tongue and hands in order to make the dancer attractive to the eyes of the public. It is not only on this occasion that dancers pray for success; before every performance they make small offerings to the deities of the dance.

Right: The *legong*, for which this girl is dressed, is often said to be the finest of all Balinese dances. Three little dancers, usually portraying an air of infinite boredom, sit on mats in front of the orchestra. They are dressed from head to foot in silk overlaid with glittering gold leaf and on their heads they wear great helmets of gold ornamented with rows of fresh frangipani blossoms. The girl who sits between the two *legongs*, their attendant or *tjondong*, waits until the moment is right, then to the accompaniment of the *gamelan* orchestra gets up lazily and stands in the middle of the dancing space. "Suddenly," writes Miguel Covarrubias, "at an accent from the orchestra, she strikes an intense pose: her bare feet flat on the ground, her knees flexed, she begins a lively dance, moving briskly, winding in and out of a circle, with an arm rigidly outstretched, fingers tense and trembling, and her eyes staring into space. At each accent of the music her whole body jerks; she stamps her foot, which quivers faster and faster, the vibration spreading to her thigh and up her hips until her entire body shakes so violently that the flowers of her headdress fly in all directions. The gradually growing spell breaks off unexpectedly and the girl glides with swift side-steps, first to the right, then to the left, swaying from her flexible waist while her arms break into sharp patterns at the wrists and elbows. Without stopping, she picks up two fans that lie on the mat and continues dancing with one in each hand, in an elegant, winding style."

Overleaf: Images of Bali, a kaleidoscopic culture where children are reserved a special place close to the gods.

HISTORY

"Bali is neither a last nor a lost paradise, but the home of a peculiarly gifted people of mixed race, endowed with a great sense of humour and a great sense of style—and with a suppleness of mind which has enabled them to take what they want of alien civilisations which have been reaching them for centuries and to leave the rest."

Beryle De Zoete and Walter Spies,
Dance and Drama in Bali, 1938

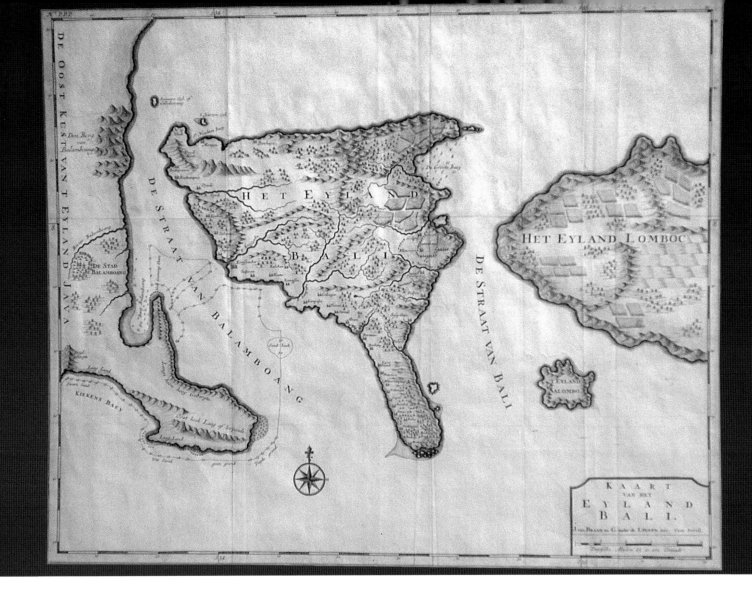

As a pearl develops from a single gritty core, so Bali's culture has grown from a nugget of indigenous belief, on to which has been slowly layered centuries of Javanese, Buddhist and Hindu civilisation. This grafting on of alien civilisation to animist beliefs has given us the Balinese culture which we know today.

As early as several centuries before the birth of Christ the island is thought to have been populated by herders and farmers, people who used bronze and iron to make implements and jewellery—early grave sites found in the mountains have revealed ancient stone seats and altars, as well as coffins sculpted in the shape of giant turtles. Certainly these people engaged in some form of ancestor worship, but beyond that little is known about Bali's first inhabitants, except that they were probably descended from migrants who moved south from Yunnan in China over a period of several thousand years BC.

Today some Balinese communities still claim ancestry from those early migrants. Called Bali Aga, or Bali Asli, they continue to live in villages isolated and independent from the general island system. These clans—one based in Trunyan on the shores of Lake Batur, another in Tenganan close to Candi Dasa, and the third at Sembiran on the northern coast near Tejakula—maintain a mountain aloofness from their fellow Balinese that sometimes borders on the brusque. The Tenganan clan still forbids marriage outside the village, a ruling which seems destined to ensure their gradual demise; the one at Trunyan shuns the conventional cremation rites of the rest of Bali and instead leaves the bodies of its dead to decompose on a ceremonial hillside next to Lake Batur.

Of the few clues to the island's early pre-history perhaps the most noteworthy is the "Moon of Pejeng", a huge bronze gong now enshrined in a temple at Pejeng near Gianyar. Still considered to have living power, this magnificent two-metre long kettle-drum is decorated with frogs and geometric motifs that probably originated from an area around Dongson, in northern Vietnam. Again, no-one really knows how the drum arrived in Bali, or when—yet the Balinese believe it to be a thing of magic,

Previous page: Bali, around 1720, as depicted by Dutch cartographers. Photograph courtesy of *Antiques of the Orient*.
Opposite: Goa Gajah, the 11th-century elephant cave, so-called because reliefs carved around its mouth were at first thought to resemble elephant ears. The cave is thought to have been created during the period of Bali's first contact with the Hindu and Buddhist population of Java.
Right, top: Funeral temples cut into the rock at Gunung Kawi, a complex of royal monuments dating from the 11th century. The site is thought to be connected to the East Javanese King Airlangga, who was of Balinese descent.
Right, middle: Fountains at Goa Gajah, which was discovered by archaeologists in 1923.
Right, bottom: Rock reliefs at Yeh Pulu, dating from the 14th century. Close by is a sacred well, but little is known about the carvings.

one of the *subangs,* or decorative ear plugs of the moon. Long ago, according to local lore, the *subang* fell to earth and disturbed some thieves. One of them, braver than the rest, climbed the tree where the *subang* had been caught and urinated over it to try to extinguish its bright light. The thing promptly exploded, killing the thief, and fell to earth in its present shape.

In spite of the "Moon of Pejeng" discovery, many scholars believe it was only with the advent of writing, imported from India via Java, that any reliable evidence of Bali's early history begins to emerge. Bali's contacts with the Hindu and Buddhist population of Java—which had already been influenced via trading passages from India and China—is thought to have started around the 8th century AD. At this time relations between Java and its smaller neighbour were friendly, a situation that was to continue more or less right up until the 11th century. By the middle of the 13th century, however, Bali had been vanquished, if not entirely colonized. By the 14th, it was brought entirely under the kingdom of King Hayam Waruk, a famous ruler of the mighty Majapahit empire that dominated East Java from the end of the 13th century until the 16th.

As a direct result of this occupation, a number of Javanese nobles and courtiers are believed to have been sent to Bali, taking with them their dances, their caste system and a variety of ceremonies which were assimilated into the rich tapestry of indigenous beliefs and rituals. To this day, Bali is dominated by a

Opposite: The Bale Kambang floating pavilion in front of the old palace at Kerta Gosa, Bali's former centre of justice. The palace was also the site for the mass ritual suicide during conflict with the Dutch colonialists in 1908.
Right: Balinese royalty at the turn of the century. The *kris* or sacred dagger holds a mythical place in the island's culture.

AUX INDES NEERLANDAISES

caste system that can be attributed to the Majapahit period: Despite Indonesia's latter day status as a republic, most Balinese people still recognize the four classes of *brahmana*, *satria*, *wesia* and *sudra*. Those who did not want to participate, we are told, fled to the mountains, where they became Bali Aga, or "mountain people".

As Islam began to establish itself in Java, so the Javanese courtiers and their families, along with other remnants of the once mighty Majapahit kingdom, became more established in Bali. By the 18th century they had begun to form separate realms; a hundred years later they had divided the island into nine great territories that still exist today as the major administrative regions: Karangasem, Klungkung, Bangli and Gianyar in the east and central regions; Buleleng in the north; Mengwi, Badung and Tabanan in the south, and Jembrana in the west.

It was in this context that early European traders and adventurers found the island during their quests east in search of wealth and territory. One account, from the 1595 voyage to the Indies by Cornelius de Houtman, described meeting with the "king", a man who sat "on a platform around three feet above the ground", and who had "around fifty deformed men, both dwarves and other types, who from their early years [had] their legs and arms bound, so that they [had] postures like the figures on the hilts of their poniards". This same king also had 200 wives and a chariot drawn by a pair of white buffaloes.

Later came the traders of the Dutch East India Company, "an organisation", says the Mexican writer, Miguel Covarrubias, "whose goal was the unlimited exploitation of the islands". The VOC, as it was otherwise known, promoted wars, seized lands, established monopolies of opium and collected revenues from the Balinese that were even greater than those exacted by local princes. The traders did everything possible to gain favour with these Balinese Rajas, but the Balinese remained aloof from Dutch attempts to control the islands. One by one, however, the regions came under Dutch control, and by 1908, following the now famous *puputan* or mass ritual suicide of around 2,000 Balinese who faced certain defeat at the hands of a large Dutch army, the island had become wholly and officially under Dutch rule.

Following its colonization, the island was administered from Jakarta, although most of its beliefs and practices were allowed to continue unhindered. Tourism began to flourish as the KPM steamships brought travellers from Europe and America, but the industry came to an abrupt halt with the landing of Japanese soldiers in Sanur in 1942. Following unsuccessful attempts by the Dutch to recolonize Bali in the wake of World War II, the island remained practically closed as Indonesia's struggle for independence took hold. Bali remained locked tight right up until the late 1960s, during which time Indonesia underwent major internal power struggles that left hundreds of thousands dead. Bali was heavily involved in the political upheavals that pitched Nationalist against Communist, and many who lived here were killed or executed as the island was purged. It may seem hard to believe, but in spite of Bali's image as an earthly paradise, its rivers have often run thick with blood.

Opposite: The *puputan* or mass ritual suicide in Badung, as depicted by a French weekly magazine of the day. The Balinese refused to fight, walking instead into the Dutch guns, or spearing themselves and each other with their ceremonial daggers.
Right, top: The Raja of Gianyar with Dutch officials and their wives taken during the 1930s.
Right, bottom: A vintage 1930s portrait of the eight Balinese Rajas gathered in the Gianyar palace grounds.

THE ISLAND

"Bali belongs to the Gods. The inhabitants are no more than transitory tenants of the land, who cultivate it and are nourished from its yield during the short span of the body's residence on earth. People die, but the earth remains—the property of the gods."

Jane Belo,
Bali: Temple Festival, 1953

A local prince and well-known Balinese doctor once showed me photographs of a landscape so barren it was impossible to believe this was the same island thousands know today as a tropical utopia. Instead of the rich texture of equatorial plants and rain forest, the black and white pictures showed a scene akin to the wintry wildernesses of Alaska, or the post-Armageddon desolation of Hiroshima. Here, in this sorry place, a solitary pair of leafless trees punctuated an otherwise featureless slope.

How could this be, I asked?

"The photographs were taken in 1963," replied the good doctor, "after the eruption of Mount Agung."

No wonder the Balinese believe that it is here, at the top of the island's highest volcano, that the gods surely dwell. To sit at the mother temple of Besakih beneath the scarred slopes of this awe-inspiring mountain is to come close to understanding the Balinese fascination with celestial existence. At turns beautiful and threatening, this mighty volcano represents a central axis around which all life—and death—revolves. When Agung blew its top in 1963, a series of vast mud flows comprising boiling volcanic ash killed 1,500 people, left 85,000 homeless and laid waste irrigation networks and rice fields created over many hundreds of years.

And today she looks so peaceful—even beautiful. Gunung Agung, at 3,142 metres, is the highest of Bali's mountains and

Pages 22–23: Mount Aguna, the centre of Bali's magical universe. **Previous page**: Life beneath the volcano—the angry mountain last erupted in 1963 during Eka Dasa Rudra, the most sacred of all Balinese festivals held just once every 100 years. **Below**: Rice has been grown beneath the volcano's slopes for at least six centuries. Bali's magnificent deer-like cattle are still used to pull the ploughs. **Opposite**: Hand-sculpted to fit the contours of the land, the island's emerald rice terraces have helped transform Bali into a verdant paradise.

volcanoes and one of the largest manifestations of the collision between the Indo-Australian tectonic plate to Bali's south and the Sunda plate to the north. Mount Batur (1,717 metres), to the west of Gunung Agung, also remains active, although its more frequent eruptions have resulted in less violent results than those of its larger cousin.

Within a spectacular crater measuring 15 kilometres across, the smoking pyramid of Batur's most recent wart-like cone sits above a glassy lake. To descend into this vast volcanic saucer is to understand what it feels like to be cut off from the mortal planet. Once inside, it is easy to believe the universe begins and ends at the darkened lip which surrounds you on all sides.

Like that remote valley, the island of Bali, with its sometimes

dangerous current-threaded seas, exists within a universe of its own. Surrounded on all sides by Islam—Indonesia is the largest Muslim country in the world—it lives as a solitary but many-sided jewel, channeling the influences of an ancient culture into a highly concentrated form. Within this universe, the island's people have created their own rules of alignment, doctrines that continue to exist today and which govern everything that they do.

Bali shuns conventional wisdom and instead maintains a proud orientation to the ever powerful mountain. Villages are laid out on an axis in line with the volcano; the sacred family temples that exist in every Balinese compound are placed in the corner closest to it. To the south—or more accurately towards the sea—a village will place its cemetery. When sleeping, a person's head—a spiritual representation of the mountain itself and therefore sacred—lies in its general direction. The feet—like the forbidding seas that lie beneath the mountain—point away from its slopes. Just like the ancient Greeks, the Balinese believe the volcano to be the representative of a more advanced form of life, one that can determine whether a crop fails or flourishes, whether a family suffers hardship or enjoys success. Only through offerings and ritual worship can the powers that live at the head of this mountain be placated.

On a more prosaic level, it is from the slopes of Gunung Agung and its sacred brethren (including the great lakes) that another central aspect of life in Bali arises: Water. This water, considered sacred when blessed, is central to the lives of the island's people. Harnessed through a sophisticated system of canals and irrigation channels that allow Bali's rice crop to maintain high levels of productivity, it provides nourishment and

wealth for all concerned. Ancient village rice-growing organisations—called *subak*—are empowered to control this precious resource. They ensure a correct flow of the fluid to the terraced fields and make sure everyone is provided with enough water to grow their crop before the flow continues down the line to the next village. And beyond.

Not all of the island's land is cultivated, however. While the coastal lowlands remain a fertile triangle of rice-producing terraces, the north subsists on lower rainfall; in the west, an unpopulated jungle, once home to the Balinese tiger and comprising nearly 20 per cent of Bali's land area, provides Bali's last wildlife sanctuary. To the extreme south, on the limestone fringes of the Bukit Peninsula, a dry and difficult terrain is characterized by impressive cliffs and caves. And across the sea to the east, this limestone terrain continues on the islands of Ceningan, Lembongan and Penida—satellites to the mother ship Bali.

However, the mountains remain key. Like the gods which they symbolize, these vast, sometimes angry cones are capable not only of taking life, but of giving it, too. Just as Agung's ash killed so many in 1963, so the same material brings fertilizing life to the island's soil. Like the overlords of a world set in a perfect microcosm, these vast mountains breathe energy into the plains and valleys, then spew out their brimstone as a terrible, biblical warning against complacency. I wonder: isn't that worth worshipping?

Left: Depictions of Bali's pastoral life painted in the naïve style: Two details from the painting entitled "The Life of Farmers" by I Nyoman Londo.
Opposite: Rice production is controlled by the *subak*, a community of farmers who ensure every piece of land is given its share of water, carried to the fields by an intricate and ancient system of channels.

Above: Mount Batur, which sits within a valley created by the massive eruption of a long-blown volcano.
The inhabitants of this curious lost world remain slightly aloof from the rest of the island.

Above: The deep blue waters of Lake Tamblingan—this lake was once attached to its neighbouring lake, Lake Buyan, until a landslide split them in 1818.

Left: The black sand coastline stretching up to Candi Dasa, to the east of the island. Many scholars claim the Balinese fear the sea, possibly because of its position at the foot of their sacred axis, where demons and devils are said to dwell.

Right: Bali's rugged limestone cliffs at Ulu Watu are a haven for seabirds and photographers. It is in this area that some of the best surfing is to be found on the island.

Above: Situated on the westernmost tip of Bukit Badung peninsula is the 11th-century Pura Luhur Ulu Watu perched above the sea. This is one of Bali's six important *sadahyangan* temples, and is remarkably well-preserved, due to the fact that it is constructed from hard, dark gray coral stone.

Above: Fishing boats at the village of Amed on Bali's east coast. Like other coastal areas in Bali, the village is largely populated by Muslims, living off fishing and salt production.

Left: Bali's beaches have increasingly lured holidaymakers to the island. Nusa Dua (top) comprises an enclave of five-star hotels, while the beaches near Padangbai, near Karangasem (below) are much quieter.

Opposite: In spite of the traditional Balinese reluctance to look seawards, some areas of the island today thrive on the fishing industry. Seventy per cent of Bali's catch is made up of the Indonesian oil sardine, *Sardinella longiceps*, 20 per cent by tuna and mackerel, and the remaining 10 per cent consisting of shark and coral fish like red snapper and grouper. Boats vary from one, two and three-man *jukung*, small enough to be hauled up onto the beach after a day's fishing, and the larger *prahu*, pictured here at Jimbaran.

RELIGION & RITUAL

"No mountain or hill, no beach, no lake or river, no forest or great tree, no village, no quarry, no palace or home, no place of cremation or burial ground is without a temple—always open to everyone, where the roof is an always shining heaven, where trees always strew flowers and where gentle breeze in the branches creates sublime music."

Gregor Krause,
Bali 1912: Photographs and Reports, 1920

"Do you believe in God?"

We were sitting, my Balinese landlord and I, on the floor of his house in Sayan, close to the town of Ubud, where painters and sculptors ply their trade amid deep green rice fields and steep river gorges. I wanted to rent his house; he needed to make sure I was a suitable occupant.

"Do you believe in God?" he repeated. "I need to know before you rent this house."

He was dressed, like the rest of the village that day, in his temple clothes—an immaculate picture of white and gold, his cloth headdress set off by a sweet smelling *cempaka* flower tucked in the folds of cotton cloth around his crown. In the background I could clearly hear the delicate tapestry of the *gamelan* orchestra playing for the temple ceremony.

"Yes," I said, "I believe."

"Good!" he said with a flourish. "Then we will be friends."

Not to believe in some kind of God in Bali would be deeply disrespectful, not perhaps to its people—they have long known the foibles of doubting outsiders—but to the sheer serenity of the island. Only a Philistine could stand on a grassy ridge between a pair of

deep rivers, look out across the land to a perfect conical volcano, or across to the shining sea, and not feel a twinge of spiritual awareness. For the Balinese, to do so would be to live as an empty vessel, devoid of all thoughts and feelings.

Even today, with the threat of mass tourism knocking at the door of Bali's spiritual well-being, the island remains intrinsically religious. Not a day passes without a ceremony taking place. Not a single shoot of rice is planted without the correct offerings first being made. Life, death, rebirth... the Balinese way of defining the cosmos is a humbling lesson in cosmic balance, an aesthetic orchestration of the often irksome questions which occasionally trouble all minds. Where are we from? Where are we going? What should we do while we are here? The Balinese have a few answers which they have made all their own.

They call it Agama Hindu Dharma, Religion of the Hindu Doctrine, and it represents an amalgamation of elements from both Hinduism and Buddhism, mixed in with pre-Hindu indigenous customs. Some time between the 8th and 15th centuries, Hinduism and Buddhism arrived in Bali from India and Java and were blended with prevailing animist beliefs, producing a colourful mixture of ritual and doctrine that is dominated by the great Hindu epics—the *Mahabharata* and *Ramayana*—and the Hindu trinity of Brahma, Vishnu and Siwa. Thus, all Balinese rituals, be they cockfights, tooth filings, cremations or others, are symbols of the constant cleansing process necessary for the maintenance of the cyclical balance of life, death and reincarnation.

Daily, this cycle and the beings involved in it are honoured by the Balinese, a people for whom life is religion and religion is life. A pantheon of gods and demons, ever present in Balinese

minds, are lauded with offerings that range from the simple to the elaborate: a few grains of rice placed on a tiny square of banana leaf at the foot of a house; a procession of towering cones of fruit borne on the heads of *kebaya*-clad women. Being gifts to higher souls, these omnipresent offerings are created with much care and dedication. There are literally hundreds of different types ranging in size and content depending on the occasion. Each is used in conjunction with holy water and the chanting of mantras to maintain a balance between the ever present forces of good and those of evil.

Previous page: The entire village attends all important temple festivals, with fines for those who fail to show.
Opposite: Prayer time within the walls of a temple is a surreal experience—a kaleidoscope of day-glo colour. Married women wear their hair in a bun; unmarried girls may let a lock of hair fall loose.
Below: A *pemangku*, or lay priest, officiates at most ceremonies on the island, chanting mantras and dispensing reverence to the gods. The right hand is considered "clean", and is used for all contact with matters holy.

Ceremonies occur all around. As part of a complicated succession of worship, each of Bali's innumerable temples celebrates an anniversary once every 210 days. In a six-month period, a family may celebrate half a dozen temple birthdays, a festival in the house temple, and three, four or five large temple feasts. Weddings, cremations and tooth filings are extra occasions for festivities. Once a year, the whole population celebrates Galungan, when the gods are invited to earth, the villages are decorated with towering bamboo *penjors*, and plays, processions and *gamelan* shows are held in all villages.

None of this is undertaken because of Bali's appeal to international tourism—in spite of our modern age, the island still reverberates to the rhythm of an ancient world, one which takes little heed of how it looks from the outside. Fortunately for us, we see it is good, and we come to watch.

Yet for the outsider, the Balinese calendar of worship can appear startlingly complex, comprising as it does both a lunar calendar—each month starts on the day after a new moon, with the full moon occurring in the middle—and the 210-day ritual cycle. The lunar calendar is based on that used in parts of India and numbered from the founding of the Indian Saka Dynasty in AD 78, so that the year 1900 in Bali began in 1979. The 210-day *pawukon* cycle is indigenous to Bali, however, and differs from other calendars in that its dates are not measured as years—perhaps because it has its roots in the growing period for rice. The

Opposite: Pura Bukit Sari temple at Sangeh's Monkey Forest and (left), one of its cheeky inhabitants. As with any temple, the sacred site only truly comes alive during its *odalan*, or "anniversary". This one dates from the 17th century.

pawukon cycle is subdivided yet again into a number of shorter cycles, which run concurrently. These comprise a number of three, five and seven day "weeks" which have no correlation to conventional time but are used to determine holy days. Each day is said to have its own god, constellation and omen indicating good or bad times for activities ranging from construction to cremation.

What could be a better illustration of Bali's on-going dedication to religion and ritual than Nyepi, the island's Day of Silence? The afternoon before this extraordinary annual festival, excited children create vast figures in demonic designs—these ogres with their long talons and fierce teeth will later be lifted onto the shoulders of groups of men and danced around the streets in a milieu of noise and colour. The festivities reach a chaotic climax before midnight, when crowds pick up and bang on drums, wooden logs or musical instruments, to be followed in the morning by a deafening silence, a time when the people stay in their houses, lights and fires are put out and the roads are made empty. This, more than any other ceremony in Bali, shows the island's true regard for ritual: the island's visitors, just like anyone else, are forced to stay inside in observance of Nyepi. For 24 hours, Bali stands silent, its beaches, bars and restaurants closed against daylight in the hope that evil forces will be tricked into leaving its deserted streets. Another ritual cleansing is taking place, this time one in which everyone is forced to participate.

Opposite: Tanah Lot, the "temple of the earth in the sea". Poisonous black sea snakes are said to guard its entrance.
Right, top: A young Balinese girl makes an offering at the sea.
Right, bottom: A temple custodian or *pemangku* checks a temple before a ceremony. Spirit houses are dressed in yellow cloth to signify the presence of holy forces.

Opposite and right: Bali's offerings take on a myriad different forms, part of the ritualistic art of the island. Simple offerings are presented daily to the gods—they may range from a tiny piece of banana leaf holding a few grains of rice to elaborate palm-leaf trays containing flowers and betel nut, a token of hospitality for the spirits. In 1937, Miguel Covarrubias, whose book *Island of Bali* is regarded by many as the definitive text on matters Balinese, wrote that offerings "are given in the same spirit as presents to the prince or friends, a sort of modest bribe to strengthen a request; but it is a condition that they should be beautiful and well made to please the gods and should be placed on well-decorated high altars". The size of the offering may also be scaled up or down depending on the occasion or nature of the "request". *Pula gembal*, consisting of dozens of different rice dough figurines, may range in size from a single basket to a spectacular construction several metres high. Women and girls nearly always carry towering cones of rice cakes, fruit and sweet breads to the temple where the gods are said to consume their essence, leaving the food intact to be returned home later. No part of the offering may be used again, meaning the *banten* must be reproduced for every single festival.

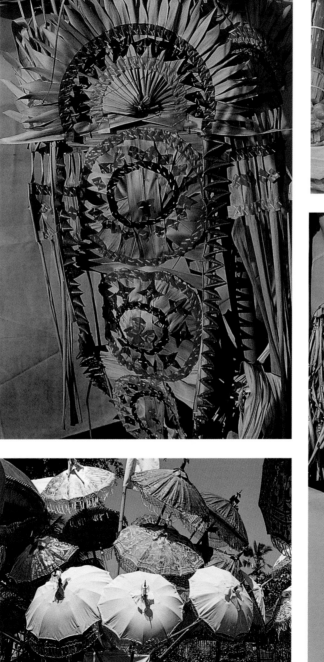

Above: Cili, the rice goddess, is a familiar shape within many different types of offering, while colours and other shapes often represent the Hindu Trinity—red for Brahma, green or black for Vishnu and white for Siwa.
Opposite: *Pula gembal*—these rice dough offerings can stand up to three metres in height for important rituals, like perhaps the tooth-filing ceremony, in which men and women have their incisors shaved to ensure entry into the next world.

Left and opposite: "Religion is everywhere in Bali," wrote Gregor Krause, a young medical officer sent to Bali by the Dutch army in August, 1912. "It is the foundation of all the pleasures and duties of man. It causes all laws to descend from Heaven to Earth, it allows nobody and nothing to feel alone. Each duty is divine, each place holy, each hour sanctified, every exterior feature is spiritually connected with the inner life." Krause spent only 18 months on the island, yet he proved a perceptive observer of Balinese life. He wrote: "Since their religion is their most vital possession, the Balinese allow themselves to be completely tolerant of other faiths. When Muslims settle in Bali, they can follow their religion undisturbed." These days it is the Muslim faith which has proved tolerant—Indonesia's constitution provides for freedom of worship throughout the archipelago, allowing Bali to continue its faith in spite of its position as part of the world's most populous supporter of Islam.

This tolerance of other faiths has caused the odd problem—when a 19th-century Dutch missionary on Bali managed in 18 years to convert just one man, his Balinese servant, to Christianity, his Church sent two other pastors to assist him. Unable to find any more converts, however, one of the new arrivees rounded on the hapless man, concentrating all his religious zeal in his direction. The servant—shunned by his Balinese peers and unable to tolerate the Christian rantings any longer—finally hired a pair of murderers who hacked the unfortunate missionary to death. When caught, he was paraded through the villages and then beheaded. Worried before the execution that his crime might bring disgrace on his fellow countrymen, he explained to them that he had converted to another religion, and thus could not be considered a genuine Balinese.

Opposite: This temple, one of the many old temples located along Sanur beach, now lies within the grounds of the Bali Hyatt hotel. Priests still come here to pray.
Above: Rangda, "queen of the *leyaks* (witches)...the most blood-thirsty, child-eating...witch widow mistress of black magic". (Miguel Covarrubias, *Island of Bali.*)

Above: The *barong*, a mythical beast said to act as protector of the village, and manifestations of Rangda, queen of witches.
Opposite: Trance in Bali is still widely practised, where the edges of reality are often blurred.

Above and opposite: A cleansing ceremony, or *melasti*, during which villagers make their way to the seashore to honour ancestral spirits. This one takes place annually at Sanur beach.

Left: The 1973 funeral of Cokorda or "Lord" Raka Sukawati of Ubud was a major event in recent Balinese history—up until the end of the 19th century, the Sukawati family remained an important princely house on the island and today still commands respect as a leading family in the Gianyar province. Unlike many royal houses which were reduced and weakened by colonial occupation, writes Michel Picard in *Bali: Cultural Tourism and Touristic Culture*, the Ubud clan managed to maintain most of its power and influence thanks to a dexterous policy of allegiance to the island's new masters. Even in today's republican Indonesia the Ubud nobility continues to play a major role in local affairs.

It was at the invitation of Cokorda Raka Sukawati that the German painter and musician Walter Spies first came to the island in 1925, and it was in the royal household that Bali's most famous expatriate first set up house—with his piano, bicycle and butterfly net—when he decided to move to Bali in 1927. At that time Ubud was better known as a centre for performing arts than for its painting and sculpture. It was dancers from Ubud and the neighbouring village of Peliatan, led by Cokorda Raka, who were to represent Bali at the Colonial Exposition in Paris in 1931, an event which for the first time established the island as a tourist destination.

Left: The cremation itself was a lavish affair that brought many hundreds of onlookers to the town. All visitors are welcome at Balinese funerals—the number of outsiders present is often seen as a measure of the importance of the deceased. Here the body of the Cokorda is carried from the funeral tower to the cremation site, where it is burnt along with an 11-tiered pyre that marks the ritual as a royal gathering. People of more humble caste are cremated with a much smaller pyre, but with no less revelry. Balinese cremations are generally happy affairs, as it is believed a show of grief disturbs the spirit of the deceased and prevents it from leaving the body. Arak, the local palm or rice liquor, and brem, a kind of cider also made from rice, often flow freely at these events, fuelling the bearers who twirl and twist the funeral tower at each crossroads in order to shake of recalcitrant demons. The whole experience, writes Clifford Geertz, a recent observer on Bali, is "a bit like a playful riot". For his part, Mexican writer Miguel Covarrubias noted: "Strange as it seems, it is in their cremation ceremonies that the Balinese have their greatest fun."

Opposite: The Cokorda's body, hidden within the bull-like sarcophagus, is reduced to ashes that are later scattered in the sea. Because of the high cost of funerals in Bali, many commoners wait until a member of the higher castes is cremated, at which time the bodies are exhumed from temporary graves and burned as part of the larger ritual.

ARTS & CRAFTS

"Everybody in Bali seems to be an artist. Coolies and princes, priests and peasants, men and women alike, can dance, play musical instruments, paint, or carve in wood or stone."

Miguel Covarrubias,
Island of Bali, 1937

The patient artisan, his face a picture of happy indifference, sits with the *paras* stone block between his feet, a hammer and chisel occasionally chipping away at the soft grey rock. First he fashions the solid column into the roughly hewn shape of a child-sized figure, the face little more than an angular muzzle, the body—are they wings?—a pair of pointy triangles. And there it sits for a day or two, alongside a dozen other faceless and similarly unfinished figures, waiting for another saronged craftsman to take up his tools and finish it off—to give it life. Finally, as he works his magic on the statue, a face appears from the rock's misty curves to become a perfectly fashioned goddess, complete in every single serene detail, right down to the impossible curve on her long-nailed fingers.

And all this, you note with incredulity, beside a busy main road in Batubulan, where the next door shop is selling aluminium washing lines and show cabinets for tourist trinkets.

No wonder Miguel Covarrubius wrote that "everybody in Bali seems to be an artist". They do, even today. Even when making aluminium washing lines. How many times have I stared wide-eyed as a stone carver from our village has created a piece of intricately beautiful work with no more effort than it takes to go to the village shop to buy a pack of clove-scented cigarettes? It seems to me that the practice of sculpting and painting in Bali is an inherent one, so much so that one could be forgiven for thinking that every single child on the island is born with a set of pre-ordained designs in his head and is capable of taking up a chisel or paint brush and reproducing them in every detail. Not only that, but they appear quite capable of picking up where someone else has left off and finishing the piece as it was originally conceived.

The architect and philosopher Buckminster Fuller recognized this almost innate ability within the Balinese to create. He wrote: "The sculpturing arts of Bali today are apparently genetically operative. In a new large building in Bali there is a 30-foot-high by 20-foot-wide and 10-foot-deep masonry chimney with a total external surface of 6,000 square feet. This surface was totally, intricately, and masterfully sculptured by two boys, one 15 and the other 12, all in a month's time. They had no drawings to work from. The whole intricate and complex folklore subject and patterning seems to have been comprehensively pre-envisioned."

The truth—if a dozen academics and past writers on Bali are to be believed—is that Bali's artistic endeavours are intrinsically linked to the way in which the island's culture has evolved, and survived. In the West, artists, writers, painters, are driven by recognition and fame, even money. Some claim a need to exer-

cise a muse. In Bali, say the romantics, artistic expression is a collective pastime, an amalgamation of traditional elements and standard features brought together to create demons and gods from the great stories of Hindu lore. There are no words in the Balinese language for "art", or "artist", said Covarrubias, in the same way that our own Western ideas of individualism are misplaced on an island driven by consensual thought. In Bali, claimed the Mexican writer, "a sculptor is merely a 'carver' or a figure-maker, and the painter is a 'picture-maker.'" The craftsman is anonymous, creating the twirls and figures necessary to adorn the thousands of temples and shrines that populate Bali from the top of its sacred mountain to the edges of its wide beaches. And anyway, why bother with posterity, when there is no death, just

Previous page: Bali's wood carving exploits have become big business today, a fact which I B Oka, a wood carver from Mas, takes full advantage of.
Opposite: The Kamasan style of painting, employed here on the ceiling of the former Court of Justice at Kerta Gosa in Klungkung, is considered a "traditional" art form in Bali and is thought to have been introduced to the island by Javanese royalty some time between the 8th and 11th centuries.
Below: An early depiction of cockfighting in Bali from a painting in the Court of Justice.

a passage to a different life, when the soft *paras* stone will soon turn green with moss, crack under the tropical sun, and the craftsman, knowing all this, will be summoned once more to create the correct figure for another temple gate, another shrine, or these days, another five-star hotel?

Perhaps for this reason, and because Bali is part of an ever-changing and ever-evolving culture, it is rare to find ancient styles in Balinese art and crafts. But there are plenty of instances of new styles, new efforts borne out of the influence of foreigners on Bali's way of life. While "the Balinese are extremely proud of their traditions", noted Covarrubias, "they are also progressive and unconservative, and when a foreign idea strikes their fancy, they adopt it with great enthusiasm as their own."

As with all aspects of the culture, Western artists and visitors have influenced the styles of Balinese painting and carving, leaving new schools to evolve in their own context—like the young artists of Penestanan, encouraged by Dutch artist Arie Smit to take up the brush and begin painting. Smit, who still lives near Ubud, was sketching a landscape one day in the 1960s when a 12-year-old boy guarding a flock of ducks nearby began drawing a figure in the sand. He later wrote: "I asked him whether he would like to draw on paper and afterwards use colours. We had to ask permission from his father. His father was not willing because the boy was his only son—and who would

Left, top: "Learning to Swim", 1995, by I Dewa Putu Mokoh.
Left, bottom: Detail from Ida Bagus Made Nadera's "Landscape".
Opposite: I Ketut Tungeh at the Tungeh Studio of Art, in Ubud, with some of his works.

guard the ducks? But is was agreed that I should teach the boy, and the father borrowed some money from me to hire a duck guardian.

"I never taught the boy anything but I encouraged him to draw and paint everything I could think of," noted Smit. The boy went on to develop a technique, introduced it to a nephew and then another relative, and within three years the group had grown to 25 young men.

These boys were to become Bali's famous "young artists", still painting in the Ubud area, which has become a busy centre for Balinese art, and a thriving centre for tourist shops and trinkets. Here, you will not find the artistic creations of the pastoral Bali, the paintings and statues of the temple buildings, but the art of modern Bali—good enough to behold, and beautiful to boot—but produced for the visitor. These days, Bali's "art" has moved out of the temple and into the shops, where, thankfully, it has become more accessible to the visitor—people like you and I.

Left: Although this batik *perada* or gold-painted batik originates from Java, textiles like it are often used as a backdrop to important Balinese rituals like tooth-filing ceremonies, in which the incisors are shaved flat.

Opposite: This jewelled *kris*, or ceremonial dagger, was wrought over a period of many months in which the *kris* maker or *empu* instilled the blade with a powerful magic said to protect its owner from evil. Often the metal is taken from a fallen meteorite which may add to the blade's force, as does the gold inlay on the dagger itself and the ruby-studded gold handle. This particular "kinata" *kris*, which shows the monkey warrior-god Hanuman, was sold by a royal Balinese family to raise money during hard times, and is believed to be more than 200 years old.

Opposite, bottom right: Traditional textiles like this single *ikat* are considered holy by the Balinese, representing a mark of cultural identity. Often the designs are based on stories from the Hindu epic plays, although this one, from the Gianyar region, depicts a simple flower.

Opposite, top: These 22-carat *prerai* or ceremonial fertility symbols originated from Singaraja in the north of Bali, where a royal family would have used them during ritual processions. More than a century old, they would have been held together with a golden chalice containing holy water.

Above: Wayan Cemul, former model and gardener for the expatriate artist Rudolf Bonnet, is himself an accomplished sculptor whose work has been exhibited internationally. He has provided many pieces for Bali's burgeoning hotel industry, two of which are pictured opposite (top middle and top right).
Opposite, bottom: A rock relief at the atelier home of Linda Garland.

Above and opposite: Many people seem to become shopaholics overnight in Bali. Typical tourist wares include paintings, wood carvings, mobiles, carved and brightly-painted Garudas, and a plethora of other fantastic objects.

THEATRE & DANCE

" It was during the first week that we came to a village bright with banners and streamers. In front of the temple a crowd was gathered and the sound of swift, complicated music filled the air. I pushed through the wall of people to a clearing, where at one end sat the musicians among their instruments. At the other end a pair of curtains stretched on a wire marked a stage entrance. "

Colin McPhee,
A House In Bali, 1947

If Bali's essence could be distilled down to a single enduring image—concentrated and bottled like a fine perfume—it would emerge as the picture of a young *legong* dancer standing wide-eyed and cat-like before the split gates of a finely carved temple. Her hair would be filled with the fragrant blooms of the frangipani tree; her bare feet positioned at right angles beneath a gold-flecked sarong.

Like all dance and drama in Bali, the *legong* was originally conceived as entertainment for the gods, a way to tempt members of the divine pantheon down from the heavens to mingle with the proletariat, but as audiences have changed, so this tradition has adjusted to meet the demands of the day. More than simply an icon for the island, the dance remains part and parcel of life.

Long ago, aristocratic houses took on the role as guardians of religious dance and drama, and after the Dutch conquest of the island the tradition moved to the villages and became a form of folk art, absorbing new vigour with each incarnation. As a result, Balinese theatre often involves an enthusiasm for experimentation and change, and its styles have in many instances been modified by outside influences. Perhaps the greatest illustration of this is the *cecak* (ke-chak) or monkey dance, originally conceived by the

Russian-born German artist Walter Spies, who lived in the village of Campuan near Ubud in the 1930s.

Spies was, by all accounts, a brilliant man. Invited to the island by one of Bali's leading royal princes, he set about absorbing Balinese life and culture and produced some of the greatest works of art ever to have emerged from the island. He was an accomplished musician too, and in 1932 created the now famous monkey dance for a German film company. Taking the chorus from a sacred trance performance, he added as many men as the stage could handle and worked in a passage from the *Ramayana* epic. The *cecak* remains a favourite with visitors to the island and still manages to ooze authenticity—in spite of its popularity.

Yet many of the island's dances remain inherently sacred, often seen only within the confines of the temple. The *rejang* consists of a procession of women moving in a slow and stately line towards the altar, twirling fans or lifting their sashes; the *baris* is a reminiscence of Balinese warriors in battle with the forces of evil. In the *calonarang*, Bali's early history is played out amid a cast of mythical creatures that includes the *barong*, a fanged hybrid created mid-snarl between a lion and a bear. There are literally hundreds of different dances on the island, many, like the *topeng* or mask dance, involving elaborate masks and costumes as well as years of practice.

Pages 72–73: *Wayang kulit,* the shadow puppet play, usually tells the story of a feuding royal family whose siblings are pitched against each other in a battle over lost fortunes.
Previous page: The *dalang,* or puppeteer, is a master of his trade. An apprentice will often spend years learning the intricacies of his show.
Left and opposite: Baris dancers. Their performance is rooted in the courtly rituals of war—the term refers to a formation of warriors.

shadow on the canvas. On to this screen he projects the images of a collection of well-known and often adored characters who play out epic battles between feuding families. Behind him, also invisible to the crowd, sits a small *gamelan* orchestra to provide the soundtrack. The action comes thick and fast, and beneath the adventure lie centuries-old messages of the constant need for balance between good and evil.

To learn and master a form of dance or drama on the island of Bali is to ensure the practitioner a revered position within the community, yet to become "famous" is not a traditional Balinese trait. As with all other aspects of the culture, students are taught to express the character of their roles as opposed to expressing one's true self—a distinctly Western idea. And so children learn a strictly defined set of moves and dance sequences which make them all but anonymous pawns of the audience—and the gods.

This does not make learning Balinese dance any easier. There are no fewer than 30 names listed for dance movements of the feet and legs, 16 for those of the arms, 19 for hands and fingers, 14 for the trunk, 20 for the neck and shoulders and 16 for facial expression. As many observers have noted, all must coincide exactly with the music of the *gamelan* or other orchestras, and this can be achieved only by a training so thorough that the music "enters" the pupil—like a bolt of divine possession. While European or American performers may have an "off" night, a Balinese performer will define the same evening as one in which he or she failed to find *taksu*, the spirit that turns an average dancer into a great dancer, or a plain looker into a beauty.

Above: The *gamelan*, Bali's celebrated temple orchestra, accompanies all dance performances on the island, where it forms a central part of the village community. The term *gamelan* refers not only to the instruments but to the musicians as well, who may start to learn the technique as young as 12 years old. Ensembles range in size from a simple quartet to a 40-strong *gamelan* gong.
Opposite: A *legong*. The dance is said to have been created by the king of Sukawati, I Dewa Agung Made Karna (1775–1825), who saw a vision of two angels during a deep mediation at the Yogan Agung temple in Ketewel.

Dance in Bali is not only an expression of devotion to the gods, or mere entertainment, but also a way of instilling cultural values on each generation. Certainly this is true for Bali's ancient shadow puppet plays, or *wayang kulit*. Every so often the shadow puppet play circus comes to my own adopted village—Banjar Baung on the Sayan ridge near Ubud—and a palpable excitement fills the community. Starting late at night and often running until dawn, the *wayang kulit* is a kind of mythical Punch and Judy show, enacted in shadows with an intricately more detailed plot.

Behind a white cloth screen—often said to represent the much-trammelled boundary between Bali's real world and the all-important ethereal world—a local *dalang* or puppet master sits with a microphone and a flaming oil lamp that casts an eerie

Above: *Legong* dancers prepare to perform in Bali. The role of third dancer, the *tjondong* or female attendant, was created in 1932 by Ida Bagus Boda, a famous dance teacher who added it as an introduction to the central narrative.

Above: Dancers are said to be possessed by *taksu*, or divine inspiration. There are literally hundreds of dance forms in Bali, where dance and drama form an integral part of nearly every ritual.

Top: The many faces of the island's mask dances. Top right is Rangda, the witch, bottom centre Hanuman, the monkey god. The others are from the *topeng*, a masked play dealing with the exploits of kings.
Right: *Sandaran* dancers: Impish, ethereal performers in the *barong* dance whose *legong*-like wigglings are said to replicate the butterflies in the god Indra's garden.
Overleaf: The *cecak* or monkey dance. Despite its apparent authenticity, the dance was created by German artist and choreographer Walter Spies in the 1930s. He drew on elements of the *Ramayana*, the sacred Hindu epic, and added it to an ancient chorus.

VISITING BALI

"'Isn't Bali spoiled?' is invariably the question that greets the returned traveller from Bali—meaning, is the island overrun by tourists, and are the Balinese all wearing shirts?"

Miguel Covarrubias,
Island of Bali, 1937

To a whole generation of young Australians, Bali is a sort of Asian Torremolinos, a two-week vacation option a few hours away by airplane where the food and accommodation are cheap, the nights long and the discos loud. For these Australians, Bali is Kuta, with its ramshackle roadside bars, its batik-filled shops, its body-strewn beaches and persistent, whispering touts. To these people Bali is fun in the sun, a cultureless beach camp where they can mix with their own, drink Fosters till all hours of the morning, and, in the parlance of my own British holiday compatriots, "go completely mental".

To others, the better-heeled Europeans say, or the Americans, Bali is the comfort of a luxury resort hotel. It is a free-form swimming pool with adjoining pizzeria, an open-air theatre with cultural show. It is CNN, a walk on the beach, a sunburned face and a feast in the grounds of a royal palace. It is the southern peninsula of Nusa Dua, with its manicured lawns and water sprinklers, its uniformed guards and limousine transfers to and from the newly renovated airport. It is a holiday with a difference—long sunny days on the beach, punctuated by an interesting and ancient culture.

To the Japanese, Bali is often a photo-op, or a golfing holiday, or these days even a surfing trip. It is the sunset at Tanah Lot, with its multi-layered ancient roofs, or the rocky beach-break at Medewi. It is Lake Batur, with its volcanic rim and, oddly Scottish, lava landscape. For the older among them, it is the inside of an air-conditioned coach, barrelling along a track built for pony traps. Bali is many things to many tourists—more than a million a year, at the last count.

To people like myself—and countless other romantics and lotus eaters—Bali is a special place. It is the central foothills, with its green, green rice fields. It is the inside of a temple at dawn, or a red-beaked Javan Kingfisher holding court over a river valley. It is a private house, brilliantly designed by a foreign architect and incorporating all the character of the island. It is a magical place, full of beauty and grace, a natural paradise populated by a kind and welcoming people for whom time seems happily to have stood still. It is an Island where the gods live, the Morning of the World. It is a utopia.

Like anyone else who has ever spent any time as a resident on Bali, I am constantly asked whether or not I think tourism is

Previous page: Amankila on Bali's east coast... one of dozens of up-market hotels and resorts on the island.
Above, clockwise from top left: Beach hawkers brighten an otherwise deserted beach; models on Nusa Dua beach, home of a dozen international resort chains; Legian beach, a more "in" version of its somewhat sullied cousin, Kuta; sunset à deux, Legian beach.
Opposite: Beach action in Sanur. Motor craft are banned in many parts of the island.

ruining the island. It is an age-old question: the Mexican writer Miguel Covarrubias asked the same thing back in the 1930s when he wrote the words at the beginning of this chapter. The answer, I maintain, is yes... and no. While a thousand hectares of rice fields are turned over to property development every year—much of it for tourism—there remains an innate sense of spirituality within the Balinese which many besides myself believe will see them through. Money earned from holiday-makers is used to buy new cars and televisions, new refrigerators and scooters, but it is also used to spruce up temples, to rebuild shrines and upgrade musical instruments. Speak to any Balinese person—and he could be a drinks' seller on the beach, or a prince from the highest courtly family—and you will recognize a sense of pride and belonging in their island that is quite exceptional. Many simply cannot consider not living in Bali, which, to my own disenchanted expatriate eyes, says something quite profound. Let's hope the optimists are proved right, and that Bali remains an island-asset for millions to enjoy.

I hope you find what you are looking for in Bali, as I have.

Left, top: Peter of Made's Warung, one of the best known Kuta cafés.
Left, bottom: Surf boards for hire on Kuta beach. Local surfers like Rizal Tanjung have been making waves on the international surf scene.
Opposite: Kuta cowboy and Peanuts Club owner Ngurah (left on bike) wheels out the weird and the wonderful for cameraman Luca. The "Beach Blanket Babylon of the East" still ranks up there as a sort of Australian Torremolinos.

Top and opposite: Tourism as art: The Balinese somehow manage to keep body and soul together in spite of a massive influx of tourists. The detail above is from a painting by I Wayan Kaler. The one on right is by I Made Budi of Batuan, an artist famous for using non-traditional subjects in traditional-style art.

Above and opposite: For those unimpressed by Kuta, Bali offers a selection of extravagant private houses for rent. You may even spot a superstar or two.

SELECTED FURTHER READING

A House In Bali, Colin McPhee, Victor Gollancz, London, 1947

Bali 1912: Photographs and Reports, Gregor Kraus. Folkwang Verlag,
   Germany, 1920

Bali Behind The Mask, Ana Daniel, Alfred A. Knopf, New York, 1981

Bali Profile. People, Events, Circumstances (1001–1976), Willard Hanna,
   American Universities Field Staff, 1976

Bali: Sekala and Niskala, Fred Eiseman, Periplus Editions, Singapore, 1985

Bali: A Paradise Created, Adrian Vickers, Penguin Books, Australia 1989

Bali: Temple Festival, Jane Belo, JJ Augustin, New York, 1953

Balinese Character. A Photographic Analysis, Bateson, G and M Mead,
   New York Academy of Sciences, 1942

Island of Bali, Miguel Covarrubias, Alfred A. Knopf, New York, 1937

Tale of Bali, Vicki Baum, The Literary Guild of America, New York, 1938

The Balinese, Hugh Mabbett, January Books, Singapore, 1985

The Last Paradise, Hickman Powell, Jonathan Cape, London, 1930

The Painted Alphabet, Diana Darling, Houghton Mifflin, Boston, 1992

Travelling to Bali, Adrian Vickers, Oxford University Press, Kuala Lumpur, 1994

Walter Spies and Balinese Art, Hans Rhodius and John Darling,
   edited by John Stowell, Terra, Zutphen, 1980